Man-Made Disasters

Fading Forests

The Destruction of Our Rainforests

August Greeley

Fading Forests: The Destruction of Our Rainforests
Copyright © 2002 by Rosen Book Works, Inc.

On Deck™ Reading Libraries
Published by Rigby
a division of Reed Elsevier Inc.
1000 Hart Road
Barrington, IL 60010-2627
www.rigby.com

Book Design: Christopher Logan
Text: August Greeley
Photo Credits: Cover © Nigel J.H. Smith/Animals Animals; p. 4 Christopher Logan; p. 5 © Francis Lepine/Animals Animals; pp. 5, 14, 16, 18 (globe) © PhotoDisc; p. 6 © Paul A. Souders/Corbis; p. 7 © Robert Garvey/Corbis; pp. 8–9 © Stephanie Maze/Corbis; pp. 10–11, 19 (inset top) © Lynn Stone/Animals Animals; p. 11 (top) © Juan Manuel Renjifo/Animals Animals; p. 12 © Nigel J. Dennis/Corbis; p. 13 © AP/WWP/Brazilian Institute for Space; pp. 14–15 © Fabio Colombini/Animals Animals; p. 15 (inset top) © Kevin Schafer/Corbis; p. 15 (inset bottom) © Chris Hellier/Corbis; p. 16 © Wolfgang Kaehler/Corbis; p. 17 © Ted Spiegel/Corbis; pp. 18–19 © AP/Wide World Photos; p. 19 (inset bottom) © David A. Northcott/Corbis; p. 20 (inset) © Richard Kolar/Animals Animals; pp. 20–21 © Macduff Everton/Corbis

On Deck™ is a trademark of Reed Elsevier Inc.

07 06 05 04 03 02
10 9 8 7 6 5 4 3 2 1

Printed in the United States of America

ISBN 0-7578-2454-4

Contents

Rainforests of the World

Rainforests are most often found in countries that are near the equator. About half of all of the plants and animals in the world live in rainforests. Some rainforests are 100 million years old. However, rainforests are being cut down so fast that they might soon disappear.

Rainforests Around the World

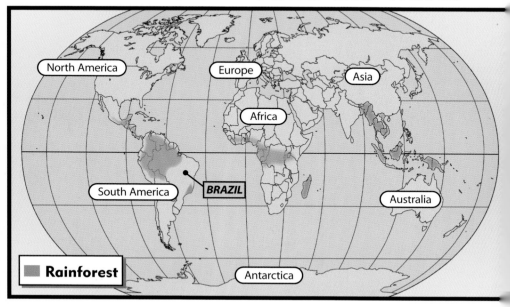

North America

Europe

Asia

Africa

South America

BRAZIL

Australia

Rainforest

Antarctica

Check It Out

The biggest rainforests in the world are in Brazil. Brazil is losing more of its rainforests each year than any other country.

Rainforest in Costa Rica, Central America

The weather is always warm and humid in rainforests. The temperature in a rainforest is between 68 and 86 degrees Fahrenheit (20 and 30 degrees Celsius).

The tallest trees in a rainforest can grow to be more than 130 feet high. Some of the trees in rainforests can live for hundreds of years.

Every year, rainforests get more than 70 inches of rain. Plants grow very well in these kinds of conditions.

Some Things We Get from Rainforests

Avocados • Bamboo • Bananas • Black Pepper • Chocolate • Cinnamon • Coconuts • Tapioca • Vanilla • Wood to make furniture and toys

Cashews and many other nuts grow in rainforests.

Destroying the Rainforests

Rainforests are harmed by some of the ways that people use them. Many farmers use a method of farming called slash-and-burn. In slash-and-burn farming, farmers cut down trees and burn them. Then, the farmers plant crops where the trees were.

After two or three years, the soil is weak and too poor for farming. It takes about ten years before anything can grow in the soil again.

Slash-and-burn farming destroys much of the land in a rainforest.

Some logging businesses use a method called clear-cutting to cut down trees to sell. When a forest is clear-cut, all of the trees are cut down and both the trees and the trunks are removed. Clear-cutting takes all of the nutrients out of the soil. Sometimes when companies clear-cut, they destroy many miles of rainforest at one time.

Once the ground is bare after clear-cutting, it takes more than 50 years for trees to grow again.

Effects of Losing the Rainforests

More than 100 species of animals and plants become extinct each week because the rainforests are being destroyed. Many other animals who live in rainforests are running out of food and places to live.

Ring-tailed lemur

Every second, a part of the rainforest the size of two football fields is destroyed. Each day, a part of the rainforest bigger than New York City is lost! Many animals that live in rainforests are losing their homes.

August 1995

May 1997

These pictures of the Amazon rainforests in South America were taken from space. The dark green in the top photo shows where thick forests once were. The red shows where forests have been cleared.

13

Many of the medicines that we use are made from plants that grow in the rainforest. If people keep destroying the rainforests, cures for some diseases may never be found.

Check It Out

Scientists think that there are about 30,000 different plants in the rainforests that have not been discovered yet. Some of these plants may be a cure for a disease such as cancer.

● This rainforest vine is used to help people who have a disease called diabetes *(dy-uh-BEE-tihs)*.

● This rainforest flower is used to treat cancer and other diseases.

15

Losing our rainforests causes great harm to Earth. When rainforests are burned and cleared, large amounts of gasses, such as carbon dioxide and ozone, go into the air.

Check It Out

If Earth becomes warmer, the ice caps in Antarctica will melt. This could cause floods all over the world.

Too much of these gasses in the air can cause pollution, a change in weather patterns, or a warming of Earth.

Trees take in carbon dioxide and give off oxygen. This adds to our air supply. Without the trees in the rainforest, there would be less oxygen for us to breathe. There would also be too much carbon dioxide in the air, causing pollution.

Saving the Rainforests

If people keep destroying the rainforests as fast as they are now, the rainforests will be gone in 100 years. Today, governments around the world are working together to stop the rainforests from being destroyed.

Check It Out

In 2001, the governments of the United States and Belize *(buh-LEEZ)*, a country in Central America, worked together to keep 23,000 acres of rainforest in Belize from being cut down.

● The ocelot *(AHS-uh-laht)* lives in rainforests. It is in danger of becoming extinct.

● Many of the birds in rainforests are dying because the trees where they live are being destroyed.

You can help save our fading forests, too! The most important ways to help are to reuse and recycle goods made from things in the rainforest. For example, using less paper means that fewer trees will have to be cut down. Together, we can save the world's rainforests.

Recycling newspaper and other things helps to save Earth's rainforests.

Glossary

acres (**ay**-kuhrz) units of measurement that are used for measuring land; one acre is equal to 43,560 square feet

cancer (**kan**-suhr) an illness caused by a harmful growth of cells

carbon dioxide (**kahr**-buhn dy-**ahk**-syd) a gas in the air that plants use to make food

disease (duh-**zeez**) illness

equator (ih-**kway**-tuhr) a make-believe line around the center of the earth

extinct (ehk-**stihngkt**) no longer living; died out

humid (**hyoo**-mihd) wet

medicines (**mehd**-uh-suhnz) things, such as drugs, that are used to treat illnesses

nutrients (**noo**-tree-uhnts) minerals that plants and animals need to live and grow

ozone (**oh**-zohn) a form of oxygen found naturally in the stratosphere that is a poisonous gas

recycle (ree-**sy**-kuhl) to make old items ready for use again

species (**spee**-sheez) a group of living things that are alike in many ways

Resources

Books

The Most Beautiful Roof in the World
by Kathryn Lasky
Harcourt (1997)

The Remarkable Rainforest
by Toni Albert
Trickle Creek Books (1996)

Web Site

Rainforest Action Network: Kids' Corner
http://www.ran.org/kids_action

Index